VALLEY TO MOUNTAIN TOP

Dr. Al Jones

authorHOUSE®

AuthorHouse™
1663 Liberty Drive
Bloomington, IN 47403
www.authorhouse.com
Phone: 1-800-839-8640

Published by AuthorHouse 03/17/2014

ISBN: 978-1-4918-6473-9 (sc)
ISBN: 978-1-4918-6472-2 (e)

Library of Congress Control Number: 2014902904

*Any people depicted in stock imagery provided by Thinkstock are models,
and such images are being used for illustrative purposes only.
Certain stock imagery © Thinkstock.*

This book is printed on acid-free paper.

CONTENTS

PREFACE

I had no plans to write this book. After my first book *Reaching For Miracles* was published, I thought it would be even more rewarding to write another inspired book, but I had no idea what it would be about! Anyway I simply told God that I was available to write if He wanted me to.

That was the end of those thoughts. In the months that followed, I continued putting on the finishing touches to a Spanish textbook for students. My thoughts were also on my first novel which I had started much earlier and was eager to continue after completion of the Spanish text.

Months later, a close relative was experiencing a serious problem. It was an extremely stressful situation and I shared some of the pain. I had to do something! So I decided I would spend a day in prayer and meditation for a solution to the problem.

About half an hour after I started, when my focus had excluded everything but the problem and God, I became aware of a voice within me which clearly said the following:

"Do not focus on the problem. It is already solved. Instead, you must focus on writing a book entitled *Valley To Mountain Top*."

I was overwhelmed! Not only was I told to write a book, I was given the title! God was actually communicating directly with me! The actuality of all this was almost incredible!

I obeyed. I continued the day as I had planned, but with a changed focus – a book rather than a problem.

At the end of the day, I was even more overwhelmed. A title and a command to write! But that hardly constitutes a book! Anyway with that much direction, I took the Bible and started to make notes. I continued to do so day after day.

After I had written almost thirty pages of notes and I felt that I had read all the passages that I was led to read, I was still not very clear in what direction I should be heading, and I was uncertain about the contents of the book. However, with my notes and the title, and the fact that the original problem was solved, I started confidently to write...

HERE YOU ARE

"Man's main aim in life is to give birth to himself, to become what he potentially is, the most important product of his effort is his own personality." **Erich Fromm**

Here you are! And you had absolutely nothing to do with it. The decision was made by others for each one of us. Now we are part of the whole scheme of things, part of the universe, so inextricably bound to Nature, to the pulse of Life that we cannot successfully dissociate ourselves from it, until it decides to release us. But often we do not even want to be released; we tacitly welcome the participation and the challenge of life.

So you have found yourself with a responsibility - that of living, of encountering whatever life decides to place in your path, and you have quickly discovered that almost everything is more complex than simple. You were, consciously or unconsciously, certain of one thing, though – You had to "have a go at it."

Instinctively we took a quick glance at ourselves and a brief look at the context in which we have been placed - at the world. We had to acknowledge that instead of chaos, there is Universal Order and some social order. Therefore there are rules governing Nature as well as our own behaviours. Life is so complicated that it takes a lifetime to understand, and we as individuals, are mixed up in the complications. So the "quick glances" and "brief looks" are just the first steps to engaging in the process of comprehending our inner selves in relation to the deeper meaning of Life – that enormous puzzle in which we are the "pieces." Without choosing to be, we are interrelated with everything and everyone else.

Such is the human condition. In the face of it, we sometimes feel more helpless than empowered. We are not initially equipped with understandings, answers and solutions. We have not been prepared. In a sense each is on his own and no one else can take the other's place. There are things that only you can learn, only you can discover, only you can do, as Life unfolds. You are unique, and at the deepest level, similar to God.

Some questions then hasten to the mind: How do I fit in? How do I manage my own life? What difference do I make to the lives of others, in fact, to the world?

STIR UP YOUR THOUGHTS!

1. Are you happy that you have the gift of life?

2. Are you in control of your life?

3. What does being in control mean to you?

4. Do you believe that it's possible for you to be the best that you can be?

5. What inspires and drives you?

WHERE YOU ARE

"It was the best of times, it was the worst of times." Charles Dickens

We have done such an excellent job of conquering the big, wide world that it has become "a global village" continually exploding with information and advanced technology. We cannot help but admire mankind's progress, terrestrial and extraterrestrial, and we know too that his genius has not yet reached its full potential. So we expect even greater achievements.

In keeping with modern civilization, societies everywhere have established regulations and rules of conduct so that life can be orderly and practicable. Depending on the country in which one lives, opportunities abound for education and work, and food is not in short supply. Life spans have been lengthened, as health care became a major focus both at the individual and national levels.

But every day our televisions and radios remind us that this is not the entire world picture. Wars and conflicts are unending, and in fact, are intensifying as the world's trouble spots continue to increase. Hunger is still rampant and a life-giving basic, such as clean water, is still not accessible to all. Even in the developed world, we are still baffled as we grapple with certain diseases; and in the under-developed world, disease still controls and devastates millions of lives.

Terrorism, hatred and desperation increasingly find new outlets. Child abuse of all kinds, including torture and murder, occur daily in all societies, as perverts seem to grow in number and in the ability to outsmart us. They succeed in duping even relatives who "know" them.

Corporate crime, power abuse, and fraud are constantly surfacing. Crime is either on the increase or it fluctuates or it changes in nature, but it is ever present. Therefore the prisons are overcrowded and more are being built, while some crime will continue to go undetected and unpunished.

Corruption and political injustices flourish. Tyrants still rule and freedom still eludes so many.

My world. Your world. This is our world!

FOOD FOR GROWTH

"Better keep yourself clean and bright.
You are the window through
which you must see the world."
George Bernard Shaw

1. Do you contribute in any way to the grim world picture?

2. Do you practise the things you would like to see everywhere in the world?

3. What kind of influence do you have on others?

4. Whom do you allow to influence you?

CAN YOU ESCAPE?

"You must be the change you wish to see in the world." **Mahatma Ghandi**

Sometimes as we view our world, we feel a sense of helplessness and pessimism. There are times too when we try to shut out the "outer world" and to seek comfort in a smaller world – our country and our society. Unfortunately though, we have to acknowledge that we cannot really escape life's encounters. There is human pain, suffering and challenges wherever life exists.

Families have progressed from being extended to nuclear, and will continue to do so as single parent families increase. Also the very concept of family life is changing. Divorce rates continue to be significantly high. Teenage pregnancies have become serious, social and national concerns, and many children find themselves outside of the ideal family setting.

Illicit drug use has established niches in several communities, and the consequences are grave. In spite of our educational programmes, promiscuity continues to play a role in the spread of diseases and untimely deaths.

The list of human afflictions sometimes seems inexhaustible, but this is our reality. Poverty and unemployment, infidelity, broken relationships, rape, accidents and failures, ill health, loss of loved ones and our constant confrontations with death, that " familiar stranger", impact on our lives at one time or another, even in our little fabricated worlds.

Is there an acceptable escape route? Even more importantly, do we really want to escape or do we want to see change in our own lives and in the lives of others, and therefore in our world?

The art of living well is the indispensable tool that we all need in this mandatory school of life in our world.

NEEDS! NEEDS! NEEDS!

*"The best way to escape from
a problem is to solve it."*

1. What would help you to master the art of living?

2. Do any of the situations described relate to any of your experiences?

3. Can you do anything about it?

4. Do you want to generally improve your life?

5. How do you think you can do this?

6. What are your deepest needs?

THE QUEST

"Happiness is the highest good, being a realization and perfect practice of virtue." **Aristotle**

We should be bent on meticulously caring for the Self, protecting and developing the image in which we were made. It is our only lasting valuable possession. Fortunately, the image is indestructible, ineffaceable, and because it is always there, we can turn our faces steadfastly towards it. This is the only route to happiness.

There can be no natural escape from life. You were given the gift of life and therefore the right to be here – to play your part in the overall plan – to live, to grow, to fit into this life in such a way as to prepare you for your place in eternity. Now you have a duty to help to bring the whole plan together by cooperating with the Maker of the Plan. You and your role are critical to the execution and fulfilment of the Plan. As life unfolds each individual must squarely face life's encounters and make choices, all of which have important far-reaching consequences.

Choices! Choices for what? What is the human need? In spite of the myriads of cultural and social differences in this world, the human need can be summed up in one word – happiness. We want certain jobs because of the happiness we perceive we can get directly or indirectly from them. We fall in love, not for the pure sake of giving love, but because we think it will make us happy. Almost everything we do in our lives, we do because we believe, consciously or sub-consciously, that we can get happiness in return. This is the quest – the search for happiness. Throughout the entire journey, this is what we are all desperate to acquire, even if only in varying degrees.

A maze of choices and pathways confronts us. Many of them will not lead us to the desired goal. In fact, many of them are naturally obstacles and distractions which merely frustrate and lead us off track. Ending up on the wrong or undesired track has always been so easy to achieve. The difficulty lies in early recognition of our direction and a necessary turning around, because the wrong track becomes increasingly problematic the longer we pursue its course. It can never become the right track to the desired destination.

Often we do not welcome turning around because we think of it as a waste of time and we trust in our ability to change and make things right as we go along the same chosen, winding path, unconscious that by its very nature it cannot yield the fruits we seek.

The seeds of our efforts can so often be planted on bad, but very fertile, soil.

HAPPINESS IS......

1. What makes you really happy?

2. Do you have in mind an image of whom you want to be?

3. Is that vision the BEST for you?

4. Are you on the right path to actualizing the vision?

WHAT IS YOUR TASK?

"To be or not to be....." **William Shakespeare**

To be happy; and to contribute to the happiness of others! Perhaps it sounds simple. But it is so complex that it can take an entire lifetime to acquire the art. There are no short cuts. In fact when we avidly seek and try such methods, we sometimes retard our own progress or never move forward. Then stagnation sets in.

Happiness means fulfilment. It is related to growth and potential. Human potential is the one gift presented to all. It is to be treasured, and nourished to its fullness. Achieving one's potential is simply becoming the best that one can be. It is to be God-like. There is no higher ideal. We are fortunate in that we have a foundation – we were made in His image, so we have the capacity to be like Him! And we have been given the time to work to achieve this potential. This is what we all need, even if we do not verbalise it or consciously think of it and plan accordingly.

There are so many re-energising water spots along the human journey, but there are also numerous distractions. Sometimes our vision becomes somewhat clouded and the distractions become more appealing than they actually are. So we succumb. This is not difficult to do, and it happens often along the way. We are fallible, and there are many hurdles; but what is critical is that we never give up and never lose sight of the goal that is attainable. It is meant to be our inheritance.

The greatest hope, the greatest accomplishment, is for each one of us to reach the end of the journey fulfilled, to reach that God-like state to which we have been called. It is our destiny.

Is there any help for setting out, journeying and finally arriving? Perhaps a lamp and a roadmap? Help is always available. Even the times we stumble and fall are our own peculiar lessons, our experiences, designed to help to illumine the dark alleys, to teach and equip us for the rest of the journey.

ACTION AND PROGRESS

1. Are there distractions in your life?

2. Is there such a thing as "progress" other than "material progress"?

3. Are you as happy as you can be with your inner self – the real you?

4. Are you maturing and growing towards your potential?

ACCEPTING THE GIFT

"Gifts must affect the receiver to the point of shock." **Walter Benjamin**

There are two choices that we do not have to make – surrender or despair. We can acknowledge who we are and accept the gift of love, and the fact that we are part of a perfect plan. Human love has its imperfections. God-love is perfect. Because it is perfect, it is multi-dimensional. It is also given unconditionally, with one aim in mind – to bring each of us to a state of perfection, where there is perfect happiness.

This is a process that demands one requirement – our cooperation. Love is not blind, it is wise and active. It does not force or bully. It simply needs our acceptance, our willingness and commitment to work with it for the sole good of the beloved, the Self.

Therefore you are only ready to seriously begin the journey to fulfilment when acknowledging who you are, you see God's offer of love, and you accept it gratefully. You then return what love you feel capable of, and in doing so, you activate the greatest of relationships. Your love will grow as you travel along, and the relationship will deepen.

When you come to the realization that you are loved, you can feel a new sense of worth and importance in spite of any situation or circumstances. You are loved and cared for by Love, by God Himself. Therefore there is none more valuable than you. In short, your happiness has begun. You are finding out what it means to be genuinely loved. Cherish the feeling and revel in it.

Then plunge deeper!

I'M LOOKING FOR LOVE

1. Do you feel genuinely loved?

2. Do you generally love people, apart from family and friends?

3. What are the things that are most important in your life?

4. Why should you bother to reach out to God and to others?

SETTING OUT

"A journey of a thousand miles begins with a single step." **Confucius**

Before setting out on the journey to happiness, we must know who is setting out. Often we do not know ourselves as well as we think we do. Self-evaluation is never easy and we do not like to do it. We think we can evaluate others more accurately than we can evaluate ourselves. Condemnation is the weapon we use on others, not on ourselves. We do not relish examining ourselves, and plunging into our own innermost recesses. This is because of fear. We prefer not to look because we suspect we will not like or accept all of what is there.

But knowing who you are is the stepping-stone for becoming who you should be. There can be no ignoring of the self. It is the only material we have with which to do the work necessary for fulfilment, for happiness.

Why should we be afraid to look inwards? Fear is deceptive. We are afraid to look, not because we do not know what is there, but because we know some of it is unacceptable; we are not happy with all that is there; we do not love it. Consequently, and often unconsciously, many of us are low on self-love and acceptance of ourselves. We think we value ourselves highly when in reality we do not. Think of all the different choices you might have made if before the act of choosing, you had considered yourself as uniquely special, invaluable and inferior to no one on earth.

If we do manage to self-examine honestly, we have to acknowledge that we are not yet (not by a long shot) what we really want to be. Using our in-built criteria, the Natural Law, we know that we have fallen short. Often we feel like crying out with St. Paul in frustration:

"For the good that I would, I do not: but the evil which I would not, that I do….I delight in the law of God after the inward man: but I see another law in my members warring against the law of my mind…. O wretched man that I am!

Who shall deliver me from the body of this death?" (Romans 7:24)

Nowhere else is the human predicament summed up so aptly and universally. The admission came out of a St. Paul who had powerfully experienced life on both sides of the fence.

When we look critically at the real self-picture, we see one with which we do not always want to associate; we find it discomforting and unacceptable. And yet, strangely, this is the very picture that God looks at, and loves. He sees it all – the creases, the tears, the burnt edges, the smudges, the wrinkles, the folds, the holes, the faded colour, the ugliness – and He loves it still. He loves it enough to want to work on it, to restore it to a work of perfection.

Again one may feel like crying out with St. Paul, but this time with joy:

"I thank God through Jesus Christ our Lord." (Romans 7: 25)

STEPPING INTO THE LIGHT

1. Do you ever evaluate yourself?

2. What do you admire most about you?

3. What don't you admire?

4. What would the perfect you be like?

5. Are you working zealously towards that?

A NEW BEGINNING

*"A good head and a good heart are
always a formidable combination."*
Nelson Mandela

It does not matter at what point you are in your life. There
is nothing that has happened in the past that can prevent
you from beginning, more purposefully, a new life – one
of fulfilment and guaranteed happiness. Just where you
are is your starting point, and the best time to start is the
time that you can be sure of – this moment.

Having accepted your gift of love, you are now beginning a
love relationship with the Giver, with Love itself, with God.
For you, this makes a difference that is incomprehensible
all at once. It takes a gradual understanding and learning.
At this stage, you need to focus on how precious you are
to be perfectly loved. If you never lose sight of this, you
will want to handle your life with extreme care, and in
turn, you will also handle others correctly. Experiencing
love in its purity engenders genuine love.

So how do you begin anew?

Understanding the self is fundamental to living successfully. It is important to know our fears, our hopes, our weaknesses, our strengths, our beliefs, and our goals. All these impact on our lives whether on not we are aware of it. So it is important to know ourselves if we are to understand our behaviour and consequently make sense of our lives. This understanding is also important because there is no relative or friend who can truly know us as we know, or should know, ourselves.

But such an understanding is not simple because of the complex nature of the human being. Therefore we are in need of some help, some enlightenment. The good news is that such enlightenment is possible.

The ONE person who has a perfect knowledge of each of us is God – the source of all knowledge and wisdom. He sees all, and understands all:

"Neither is there any creature that is not manifest in His sight: but all things are naked and open unto the eyes of Him ...." (Hebrews 4:13)

"You know my downsitting and my uprising. You understand my thoughts afar off....and You are acquainted with all my ways. For there is not a word in my mouth, but lo, O Lord, You know it altogether.

Where shall I go from Thy spirit? Or where shall I flee from Thy presence? (Psalm 139: 2-7)

It is useless to deny His spirit and presence. He knows past, present and future:

"My substance was not hidden from You, when I was made in secret ....Your eyes could see my substance; yet being unformed; and in Your book all my members were formed, the days fashioned for me, when I was not even a day old." (Psalm 139: 15-16)

Therefore He is the only perfect person who has the knowledge and wisdom to help you put all the pieces together meaningfully, so that you **can be** the beneficiary, so that you can be happy, so that you can achieve your life's ultimate purpose. But is this kind of help available to you? Yes, because of your gift of love you can access it, you can "come boldly unto the throne of grace…and find grace to help in time of need." (Hebrews 4:16)

THE CHALLENGE?
A NEW YOU!

1. What are your strengths?

2. Do you have any weaknesses?

3. What can you do about them?

4. Into what /who are you trying to fashion yourself?

5. How do you respond to the fact that God knows you through and through?

IS THERE A MODEL?

"The glow of inspiration warms us; it is a holy rapture." **Publius Ovidius Nasoovid**

"Beauty awakens the soul to act." **Dante Alighieri**

You want to achieve happiness, fulfilment. You want to achieve the purpose for your life – your precious life-which is invaluable in God's eyes. You are the main person who will lose or benefit depending on how you live this life. So you should care meticulously. We know that to walk along the right path is often complex and difficult, and that as human beings we are imperfect, but we also know that we can tap into the source of Love and power to receive all the help that we need.

We have a second important gift – Time. We have the time, the opportunity to turn our lives around, to begin afresh, to improve every aspect of our lives, to be continuously improving until we reach that state of fulfilment.

As we stand again at the beginning of life's journey, or as we continue it, without knowledge of the future, with some uncertainties, doubts and fears, we should be conscious of our own shortcomings and should feel the need for some kind of a guide, a model, on whom we can focus fixedly as we travel.

All we need now or will ever need has been provided for us – even the Model. God is not flesh and blood as we are, so we "see" Him only by faith. He knew we needed a more tangible model and so Christ came into the picture with God attributes and human ones as well. He therefore can identify with us, and we with Him.

"For verily, He took not on Him the nature of angels; but he took on Him the seed of Abraham. Wherefore in all things, it behoved Him to be made like unto His brethren, that He might be a merciful and faithful high priest....to make reconciliation for the sins of people. For in that He Himself hath suffered being tempted, He is able to help them that are tempted." (Hebrews 2:17-18)

Jesus Christ is therefore our guide and roadmap to find what we need most of all.

From His life and teachings we can learn all we need to know, we can grasp all the tools we need for the task of journeying along successfully.

HELP? WHO NEEDS IT?

1. Do you need any kind of help?

2. How self-sufficient do you feel in every aspect of your life?

3. Do you ever feel that you could be a much better person in every way?

4. How much help do you give to others?

5. How do you rate Christ as a model?

IN WHOM ARE YOU TRUSTING?

"The object of the superior man is Truth."
Confucius

There is nothing that we need to know for this life that we cannot learn from Jesus Christ – The perfect God-Man, the Model, the Prime Example, who can guide us to become like Him ultimately. He has already walked the same human road. He has attained what we want to attain. He has already arrived at the place where we should be heading if we too want to achieve that fulfilment, that state of perfect happiness, of becoming who we were destined to be.

"....... As He hath chosen us in Him before the foundation of the world, that we should be holy and without blame before Him in love: Having predestined us unto the adoption of children by Jesus Christ to Himself .... In whom we have obtained

an inheritance, being predestined according to His purpose" (Ephesians 1: 4-5&11)

Such is our legacy!

The question is what should your reaction be to this kind of inheritance of supernatural magnitude. Are you willing to trust God and believe His word? A simple act of faith activates a relationship that can never spoil, a relationship which can never be broken:

"**....After that you believed, you were *sealed* with that Holy Spirit of promise**" Ephesians 1:13

Is there anyone in this life who has promised you more than God has? How should you respond to God? St Paul prayed that the Ephesians would react by being enlightened, by embracing such a call, by understanding the "riches of the glory of the inheritance" and by trying to grasp "the exceeding greatness of His power" given to those who believe. (Ephesians 1:18-19)

An acceptance of God's gift of Love and all that this entails involves basic faith. This is critical at the beginning and at every step of the way – because there will be faltering, even some tumbling and bruising. But with Faith in God your goal is attainable.

Everyone, even if only tacitly, needs someone or some people whom they can trust. Trusting is an aspect of human behaviour. Acknowledging this need we usually make our own selections. Sometimes they are good, sometimes bad. But this does not stop us from trusting – because it is a continual need.

What must we do then? When someone in whom we trusted fails us, it is not always because the person is a traitor or deliberately set out to fail us. It is simply that the person because of his/her own weaknesses succumbed to a temptation. It is important to keep in mind that those we trust can be as fragile, as confused, as weak, or weaker than ourselves. They may also be struggling along some pathway where there is not a lamp, a guide, or the needed help. We must also always remember that the kind of help others can give has its own limitations. At times we all find ourselves in need of some kind of infallible help.

As a foundation for trusting each other, we need to trust God, the One who cannot falter and will not fail us. If we trust in God and the persons we trust also trust in God, then it means that the probability of breaking that trust is negligible. The message is that we have to be careful about selecting the persons whom we trust. We must have a set of criteria – criteria influenced and established by the One who never fails. The more we trust in God, the more likely we are to choose the right people in whom to place our trust in this life. The benefit is two-fold – the more we trust in God, the better the choices we make and the wiser we become as we walk along. With wisdom comes strength.

The act of faith pervades life at all levels. We exercise some kind of faith every day as we carry out the simplest of activities – like boarding the bus or getting into a car. Faith is an innate gift. We cannot live without releasing it in varying degrees at different times in our lives. Our existence depends on it. Therefore faith is also given to us because without it we can never get close to an invisible, omnipotent, omniscient God. It is impossible to reach our target without faith.

A simple act of faith in God brings about desirable changes now and forever. Refusal to release this faith can only hinder your search for happiness, thwart your purpose in life and leave a blank in God's plan where you are concerned. It means a refusal to participate in the fullness of life, now and eternally, as God intended.

Eventually, all of us must acknowledge God:

"…Every tongue shall confess to God."

Therefore why should anyone even try to "kick against the pricks"? (Acts 9:5)

Why should time and lives be wasted when we have the perfect alternative? To what end do we ignore the perfect plan for our present and future well-being?

Our well-being, our happiness, and our real success in living are all bound up in, endemic to our relationship with God. This is so because we are made in His image; we are His, and cannot be truly and lastingly fulfilled outside of this relationship that was established for our benefit:

"…. You have received the spirit of adoption, whereby we cry, Abba, Father. The Spirit itself bears witness with our spirit, that we are the children of God. And if children, then heirs of God, and joint-heirs with Christ…" Romans 8:17

That simple act of faith in God is an acceptance of what God offers, and it opens the door to life now and to eternity. At that time, our union with God will be perfected and all of life's possibilities will become our realities.

BUILDING TRUST AND FAITH

1. Do you know anyone who is infallible?

2. Do you know anyone who has only your sole interest at heart?

3. Is anyone trying to mould you into a perfect being?

4. Do you see yourself as a child of God?

5. Who/what do you deeply believe in?

ON BEING PRACTICAL

"It is not the length of life, but the depth of life."
Ralph Waldo Emerson.

What is trust and faith in God all about? It is an acknowledgement of a God who has communicated with man through Jesus Christ. What is known about God is learnt from the teachings of Christ. So we must believe and accept Christ's words. In this single act of faith and acceptance of Christ, we are acknowledging God as Father and Saviour and are positioning ourselves to take a journey that leads to perfection and to unity with Him.

Faith is the foundation block on which we build a little each day. Without such a foundation, anything we build will not help us to achieve the goal. So faith is the starting point; and it involves the will, making a deliberate choice to believe and to cooperate with God to fulfil His purpose for you. Then there is the promise of many gifts and blessings as we travel along, so that happiness can begin immediately and then grow to perfection.

Life is made up of myriads of situations, small and great, that require us to make endless choices. The whole question of life - how you live it, where you are heading and where you will be ultimately – also requires you to make the most important choice that anyone anywhere can ever make. You cannot refrain from choosing. We all make a choice concerning this question, whether or not we are aware of it. Our actions and behaviour indicate the kind of choices that we make. It is wise to be aware of the choice because it will impact on your life forever.

Understanding who we really are will undoubtedly cause us to make some fundamental changes and adjustments. We are like God somewhere deep inside of us. To be a human being is to be provided with the highest opportunity there is to find that likeness, to treasure it, to nurture it, and to make it grow to that state where we are one with God.

A denial of who we are means setting ourselves up for failure and hurt. Denial means a refusal to select the path and accept the opportunities that will result in fulfilment. Denial means a refusal to accept the self and allow that self to live, to thrive and to grow into perfection. From the beginning of time, we have been the focus of God's care, His love and plan:

You were "redeemed with the precious blood of Christ... who verily was foreordained before the foundation of the world, but was manifest in these last times for you." (1Peter 1:18-20)

"...You are a chosen generation ...God has called you out of darkness into His marvellous light." (1Peter 2:9)

We should answer that call. There is none nobler!

CHOICES! CHOICES!

1. Do you know that all choices have consequences?

2. How can you ensure good consequences?

3. Who are the people whom you trust most?

4. What do you do daily that involves some kind of faith?

5. What might you gain if God had a place in your life?

6. What might you lose if He didn't have one?

TRAVELLING WITH BURDENS?

*"We first make our habits and
then our habits make us."*

Often we know when we are not who or what we should
be. But there is usually a tendency to ignore or to attempt
to justify our behaviour.

If there are things about you that you do not like, you are
not powerless and therefore you can change those things.
You can shed as much baggage as you really want to.

We should not want to travel along with unnecessary
luggage. It will slow us down, hold us back, cloud our
vision, sap energy which could be better utilized, frustrate
us and our hopes to move on and achieve our goal.

But what is baggage? Anything that weighs you down and
diminishes your freedom.

When someone hurts us, why do we continue to carry, and even preserve the hurt?

Why do we allow anger to bombard our systems, chip away at our hearts and minds and boost hypertension?

How long should we allow that piece of malice to eat away at our peace of mind and leave its deep stain? Often the object of our malice is not even aware of what we are doing or feeling. Therefore who is the real victim? What makes us victimize ourselves in this way?

When we hate others (who are probably not aware) what are we doing to ourselves? Why would we want to express that hatred in action? To what end?

Why must we compete on the materialistic level with others, whose situations and circumstances we do not really know? Such goal- less competition wastes us away because we are running on the wrong track, without a finishing line. Isn't our business to look after our unique self and to so fashion our lives that we reach our potential?

What benefit do we think we are providing to ourselves when in our gossip we tear others down and spread statements for which we have no proof? Why do we always forget that we cannot build ourselves up by tearing others down?

Why do we disrespect others and forget that in doing so we are also really disrespecting ourselves? Such is the nature of disrespect. It always starts inside.

Why should we feel envy and jealousy instead of sharing joy and feeling genuine interest?

Why should we be ungrateful when the more grateful we are, the more inner peace we have?

Why is there room in our lives for excess pride when we are truly as small as everybody else and Wisdom itself knows we are all the same?

After practising these things, will we admire the persons we have become? Was that our goal? How much progress did we make as a result?

Why do we allow negative emotions to turn, twist and enslave us?

Why? Why? Why? Why?

There is only one answer. We have lost sight of how precious and important we are in God's eyes. We are not accepting His love or seeing the vision of His perfect plan for our lives now and forever. Instead we have chosen not to accept and cooperate with Him. We have spurned all the gifts to our detriment and self-degradation. We have not been concentrating on making ourselves whole and fulfilled. We have not accepted that we have been given "all things that pertain unto life and Godliness"

(2 Peter 1:3)

Therefore we make ourselves poor indeed, and worse. We have not dealt justly with ourselves and we have allowed the self to further stray from the Self with all its latent power and God-given possibilities.

CHECK YOUR LUGGAGE!

1. What are some of the things you treasure most?

2. Are those things genuine treasures that can withstand the test of time?

3. What do you see as the purpose of your life?

4. How can faith affect your life?

5. How much luggage do you want to carry?

CONTINUAL SHEDDING OF OVERLOAD

"He conquers who endures." **Persius**

The task of shedding baggage should not be ignored in life's journey. In fact, it is a continuous process in the business of growth in which fallible human beings are engaged. In this sense it is like any other thriving and dynamic venture that demands evaluation, renewal, and change.

With every act of shedding the harmful, a greater degree of freedom is attained – freedom along with its counterpart, power - Freedom to choose and Power to follow through.

Although we are individuals with varying personalities, we have much in common as members of the human race. Often the temptations and the trials are basically the same in nature. Therefore we should all be on our guard, and avoid the general pitfalls that abound simply to lead us astray and to destroy us. The Bible pinpoints all of these obstacles and advises us to "set our minds on things above, not on things on the earth." (Colossians 3:2) Anything that the Bible has ever advised us to do is based on putting our well-being first, on achieving the goal of life.

Advice is not always welcome, easy to accept or to act upon. This is why the source of the advice is of such importance – we need only the advice which we can fully trust, which can never lead us astray and which has no other motive but our best interest. This advice is available as a two-fold gift, in the sense that it not only benefits you but all those to whom you relate. While you are growing, you are also influencing other people for the better.

God encompasses all virtues. He is the epitome of all goodness. Hence we can look to Him for guidance as we seek to let His image in us find expression and development. There are some things we are told to "put off" and some things we are told to "put on". So the gear we wear along the journey is important. Some of the things from which we should protect ourselves are listed in Colossians 3. Some examples are sexual immorality, greed, anger, wrath, malice, dishonesty, blasphemy and any kind of evil which the conscience, that watch dog, may indicate to us. Is it possible for anyone not to see why we are told to avoid these things? Emotional, mental and physical anguish are some of the prices that many people have paid.

As human beings, made in God's image, we often know the difference between right and wrong. We have an in-built alarm system activated by sin – the word we do not like to hear, the word that tends to make us uncomfortable and drives some to try to redefine the nature of mankind all over again. However time and experience have consistently revealed our true nature. But we should not recoil from the word – sin. It is a word to keep in mind and against which we should protect ourselves. It is simply, and summarily, anything that prevents us from becoming the best that we can be, anything that does not fit into the image of God. As C.S. Lewis puts it: "***Sin is a distortion of the energy breathed into us. Therefore all sin is sacrilege.***"

The longer we practise it, the more it becomes natural to us, changing our very nature and preventing us from becoming who we are originally intended to be. Any sin committed, is a sin against the self first of all, because the self was not created to act in such a way. Secondly it affects others. In spite of any outward glamour, wrong actions always have negative consequences – some of which we are not always aware. Because sin is always destructive, we need to struggle against it. This is why we are given rules, laws, wisdom and a vision of the Christ-like self that God intended for all.

TOO HEAVY A LOAD!

1. Are you carrying useless baggage?

2. Is it necessary for you to carry it?

3. Does carrying it and dissolving it mean the same thing to you?

4. Do you want to free yourself from it?

5. Do you punish or forgive yourself and others?

CLOTHING FOR THE JOURNEY

*"Put on the whole armour of God that
you may be able to withstand...."*
St. Paul

Help is available in this area. We have only to look at the character of Christ. Two of His hallmarks are unconditional love and selflessness. Unconditional love is the kind of love which we accept from Him and which in turn we draw on in our relationships and encounters with other people – without caring who or what they are. Our treatment of them should be based on unconditional, Christ-like love. Even when this gets difficult, as it can, depending on the calibre of people we meet, we need only remember the source of Love and the fact that we are beneficiaries. Such love is the main river from which all our other activities should flow to provide the appropriate nutrition for growth and happiness. Love has been described as "the bond of perfectness." (Colossians3:14)

By being selfless, in some strange way, the self thrives and moves along the road to fulfilment and perfection. The art of selflessness involves humility, tolerance, forgiveness, mercy, kindness, patience and empathy, among other things. Imagine a new, enriched self that cultivates such qualities! Character formation has never been an easy task. The only strategy that works is practice. Such qualities will take time to develop, but we do have time as we travel along. In fact, this is the only reason that we have been given time – to develop a self born of the image of God, to be moulded and fashioned until we are as much like Him as possible. Saint Bernard once said that we are given time so that we may know God, and it makes sense to add that in doing so, we also get to know our real selves as we are and as we can be.

The journey of life is so challenging that we are told that we must put on "armour". Without armour, we can so easily find ourselves in the swirling waters where forces from every direction attack and thwart us. What is this armour? There are seven basic pieces. It begins with the foundation block of Faith. Without faith, it is impossible to imitate and become like God. Without faith, it is impossible to be victorious, to overcome and move on. Faith is described as the "***shield …with which you shall be able to quench all the fiery darts of the wicked***". (Ephesians 6:16)

Faith in God points to another important piece of armour – Salvation. This is a gift, simply to be accepted. It is part of the weaponry because with this, you receive identity, stability and in a sense invincibility because no force can take you out of that saved relationship. You are protected. Salvation is referred to as the "helmet". (Ephesians 6:17) Under such protection, you are free to work on the self and to reach your destiny, intact.

As we walk along, we are told that we need to have our "loins girt about with Truth." (Ephesians 6:14). Truth gives us direction; it guides us and helps us to see. This is critical on a journey that is not always clear and straightforward. Without Truth, deception will twist and turn us in every direction but the right one. Lives can be wasted, and goals unachieved as some find themselves at the last tragic stop on the wrong road - a consequence of not embracing truth.

In life's encounters, we need a "sword"- This is the word of God. (Ephesians 6:17). Jesus, of course, used this sword with perfect dexterity. In the face of every temptation, he countered with a quotation from God's Word. As a man, He knew it. He needed to, as we too need to know it. For us there are no greater words of wisdom, there are no greater truths, there is no better advice, there are no higher standards, there are no higher ideals. We need the Word as we journey along. It is our answer in temptation.

The truth is tied up in the Word and it is indispensable to us.

Then we need a "Breastplate". This is Righteousness (Ephesians 6:14) or goodness – something that we all think we have to some degree, something that we can become cynical about, not because we do not admire it but because we think it is too hard, demands too much effort to achieve it to the fullest degree. And yet, the self is starved and stunted when we do not practise righteousness as we should. It is the very food on which the self, the soul, is nourished. To practise goodness is essential to reaching your full potential and to finding peace with yourself and with others. So out of this practice evolves another piece of armour. It is Peace (Ephesians 6:15). Imagine a world in which everyone has inner peace and helps to create peace for all. Peace is really not that elusive after all.

From the practice of goodness and peace, benefits multiply and produce happiness, genuine joy that nothing can touch. The armour is for our protection, our joy, our very survival and our victory.

ARE YOU ARMED
AND READY?

1. Are you clear about the direction in which you are heading?

2. As you travel along, what are you taking with you?

3. Will those things help you to reach your destination?

4. Is there a Knowledge Source that will help to guide and keep you on the right track?

5. Are you fully armed for your journey?

YOUR NEW CONCEPTUALIZATION

"The depth and strength of a human character are definitely its moral reserves."
Leon Trotsky

When we look at Christ closely enough, He always inspires admiration and awe. Also He inspires confidence, trust and hope, the hope that we can become like Him. In fact He has made us many promises:

"He has given to us exceeding great and precious promises: that by these ye might be partakers of the divine nature ....."

So we will become like Him. Now we can have a new focus, the worthiest of all. It is in understanding our capability as children of God that we can live to achieve our highest potential.

When we put our faith in God, we begin to become aware of our position because of Him. We are now aware that we are children of the King, that we are so precious that the greatest of miracles (God taking on human form) took place on our behalf. So we can now assume genuine self-importance and self-worth. Faith results in change. It involves having "a new mind", an entirely new perspective. As St. Paul says in Colossians 3:10, you "have put on the new man and should walk in newness of life"(Romans 6:4). This "new man" is "created in righteousness and true holiness." It is a new mission – the highest!

But what does the new life look like? When we placed our trust in God and His word, we became free to commit to righteousness (Romans 6:18). So the new life is one characterized by goodness. All of us know what it means to do what is good. It is the act which makes the self rejoice as it is being moulded and fashioned to look more like its God-image. In essence you become more like the individual you were designed to be according to God's purpose and plan.

Surely to live a righteous life is not the easiest of tasks. However when we take that initial step of faith, God does not remain passive, He acts. Immediately His holy spirit comes to us and we are now considered His temple, His dwelling place. (1 Corinthians 3:16) He will lead us as no other can. With our permission and cooperation, God will work with us to build and to finally achieve the ultimate – *"a perfect man, unto the measure of the stature of the fullness of Christ."* (Ephesians 4:13)

Inspired by His promises, we believe, we know, that we can. For us there is no sense of failure because we know that we "are kept by the power of God through faith" (1Peter 1:5). We are given what we need to succeed. "God...who hath blessed us with all spiritual blessings in Christ." (Ephesians 1:3).

We can be confident of victory:

"Thanks unto God who always causes us to triumph in Christ."(2 Corinthians 2:14).

The human being is always growing and becoming. Therefore it is necessary to be careful about the quality of our lives which creates the end product. Our faith and our wills are the soil from which good fruit can grow. They are the ingredients that God needs to work with us to perfect our lives.

EFFORTS AND STRUGGLES!

1. How much can you achieve without real effort?

2. How much do you value what is achieved effortlessly?

3. Do you need to protect yourself from anything?

4. Are all your efforts designed to bring you good?

5. Where can you get the help you need?

THE LEGACY

"You were sealed with that Holy Spirit of promise which is the deposit on your inheritance."
St. Paul

"…The love of Christ which surpasses knowledge…" (Ephesians 3:19). This is the love that comes from the One who is the source of all life, who is omnipotent, omniscient, omnipresent, eternal, perfect, and the list can go on and on. The good news is that we are the objects of such love. It is such a miracle and a mystery that we can only learn to grasp its fullness as we grow, as our faith deepens and our understandings develop along our journey. So we are loved in full depth by Love itself. Love undergirds everything. This means that we are the recipients of more than one thing, we have an abundance from God.

Our inheritance is multi-faceted. "Therefore you are no more a servant, but a son; and if a son, then an heir of God through Christ." (Galatians 4:7) We can learn, even if it takes a lifetime, what it means to be such an heir. We are "members of Christ" (1Corinthians 6:15). The relationship, in its fullness, cannot be closer, and there is much to be derived from such a relationship.

There is a significant difference between the place where we stood before and after placing faith in God and accepting His gift of love. In fact, there are many differences, and they are all most desirable. God has "raised us up together, and made us to sit together in heavenly places in Christ Jesus." (Ephesians 2:6). We are also "fellow citizens with the saints" (Ephesians 2:19) – we who could hardly be honestly described as "saintly." It takes our faith and our imagination to try to relate to the riches of our inheritance. Its benefits begin with our faith and continue throughout the journey and beyond: *"...an inheritance incorruptible, and undefiled, and that fades not away, reserved in heaven for you."* (1 Peter 1: 4*)*

Try to imagine that in God's eyes, there is no difference between the Son Christ and you. Knowing ourselves, this seems impossible. But knowing us, God still says it is all ours, for the taking. The bible speaks of the many and various gifts and the true riches of character that God has provided for us to use in the growing process, for our fulfilment. One of the gifts is that we constantly have access to God "In whom we have boldness and access…"

(Ephesians 3:12). How many important people are there in this world to whom we have bold access?

Let us revel in God's love and wealth as we approach Him boldly, whenever we want to, and walk forward confidently to happiness and fulfilment.

YOUR INHERITANCE

1. What would you like it to be?

2. How valuable is your choice?

3. Do you see a perfect correlation between financial wealth and happiness?

4. If not, what could possibly be missing?

WALKING THE WALK

"Practice is the best of all instructors."
Publius Syrus

Here you are now with purpose, with a focus on a specific destination and some sense of direction. Now you have a better understanding of who you really are, what you can be and will be. Determination and the power of the will are two necessary tools that you should grasp and keep in use throughout the journey.

But do you have to walk alone? No. "Lo, I am with you always." This is a promise that Christ kept in spite of His physical absence. His physical presence was to be replaced by the gift of the Holy Spirit. This is simply empowerment. When a group of frightened, despondent deserters received this power, they were completely transformed. They shook and influenced the world. Their experiences, writings and their lives continue to impact on millions after thousands of years.

No. You are not alone! There is a special divine empowering presence and there are also millions of people like you who have embarked on the same journey. God can never desert you. The choice is yours to walk with Him. The grandeur of such an undertaking implies that it cannot be successfully achieved without effort. But remember you begin equipped, to some extent. You are "rooted in Him and established in the faith." (Colossians 2:7)

You have also begun to wear the pieces of armour. Whatever you are still lacking will be developed during the process of growing and becoming fulfilled.

The journey is a developmental process and there are many guidelines and warnings of obstacles along the way. The guideline that summarizes many others is to avoid all evil. Jabez, a biblical character, fully understood the nature of evil. He is mentioned only briefly in the Bible (1 Chronicles 4:10) with the short prayer that God would protect him from evil so that it would not cause pain! All evil causes pain either to the doer, to the victim, or to both. It always negatively affects the doer even if the individual is not aware of it. This is so because we were not designed to be evil. On the contrary, we are designed to be like God. So that any evil act distorts the self and prevents one from becoming what he should be. The longer one pursues a course of evil, the more distorted the personality becomes and eventually self-actualisation and fulfilment are impossible. The individual takes his twisted, stunted spirit into eternity.

Always remember that all evil is destructive. This is why God wants us to turn away from it – not because He wants us to be "goody-goody" or to spoil our "fun". He wants us to be preserved whole, to be fulfilled and to be ultimately perfect.

How does one avoid evil? In fact the question is really how does one avoid causing pain?

You can seriously begin by practising to love. This is not the warm cosy little feeling that we sometimes feel about other people. It is an art that can only be acquired by practice. Love is vast and embraces many characteristics, so many, that if we truly love, there is some evil it is impossible to commit. Love is the converse of evil. Real love is described in 1 Corinthians 13: 4-8:

Love is patient.
Love is courteous.
Love is not envious.
Love is not arrogant.
Love is slow to anger.
Love forgives and forgets.
Love is truthful.
Love is considerate.
Love is not suspicious or sceptical of others.
Love is interested in the welfare of others.
Love is supportive of others.
Love never fails.

Love is enduring.
Love is selfless.

This last trait of love may seem strange because we also need to love ourselves. But selflessness is almost an enigmatic characteristic in the sense that when we are being selfless, we are actually nourishing the self and setting it free to act in the only way that brings it real satisfaction, and gives a sense of achievement. Every selfless act brings one closer to a state of purity. Christ was the supreme example in this regard.

Love, a topic so vast, so profound, so necessary to life that it can be discussed endlessly................

I KNOW WHERE I'M GOING

1. Do all roads lead to the same place?

2. To which destination will your road lead?

3. Do you need any guidelines?

4. Do you have strategies for dealing with obstacles?

GREATER LOVE

"Love is the important flow of energy that nourishes, extends and preserves. Its eternal goal is Life."
Smiley Blanton

Love! We need so much of this – from family, friends, and even from the world. Everyone seeks it, and when the quest is fruitless, we are miserable. Even sometimes when we find it, we exact the maximum, we want it in its pure and perfect form. Seldom though, do we focus on how much love we give, on how much love we beget and share to those who need it.

In spite of the fact that we all need love, we often underestimate its power and significance. In Colossians 3:14, we are told that Love is the "bond of perfection" and we are constantly encouraged to practise it. Jesus told His disciples that Love should be their hallmark and by exhibiting love, all would automatically know that they were His followers, being moulded and fashioned in His likeness.

But why should a loving nature be so important? It is an essential for the soul. The Self cannot attain fulfilment without it. Whether we like it or not, no man is an island and we are all related. We cannot ignore others and live selfishly if we want to grow, to find happiness and fulfilment. Other people exist, not to be ignored, but to give us an opportunity to practise love, to practise being what we should be. They exist, not to bring out evil such as hatred, anger, gossip, malice, envy, dishonesty, but to bring out goodness. In short, others are there to help us grow along the journey. If this is our attitude towards people, then we would grow in leaps and bounds. According to St. Paul, Love "edifies." The one demonstrating the love always moves on to a higher level. Love is empowering and helps us to conquer.

Love can undergird everything. "For all the law is fulfilled in one word, even in this: Thou shall <u>love</u> thy neighbour as thyself." (Galatians 5:14)

This one word has been the basis of many a prayer throughout our history – that we would love God and love each other. In fact it is in loving each other that causes our love of God to flourish. Love of God and love of the other cannot be separated. It is one and the same love. We are told that if we do not love our brother, then we cannot really love God. We are also told that "If we love one another, God dwells in us, and His love is perfected in us."(1 John 4:12) The message to us to love is not new. It is an old repeated one. According to 1 John 3:11, it is "The message that you have heard from the beginning, that we should love one another."

Love is so vast that it has many by-products. Kindness is an important one. This quality which springs from love is one of its practical manifestations. It is such an admirable characteristic that we all love to see it. But it is from practising rather than seeing it that we can derive the greatest benefit. The benefits are twofold – both the giver and the receiver reap the rewards. Picture the joy and the glee from the receiver and imagine the light breaking into a smile on the face of the giver, and the feeling of warmth on the insides of both. This is just an inkling of what really happens when we demonstrate kindness. It is as if the soul is bursting new ground and exploding into its true self. Quite simply, we are growing and metamorphosing into that new being. Our purpose is being fulfilled.

At this stage of our growth, we are not only concerned with working on our outward beauty, but on an inner beauty as well – the beauty which does not fade, but brightens and deepens into perfection.

Kindness, this quality of the heart that seeks nothing in return, involves many other qualities. It involves being tolerant, tenderhearted, merciful and gentle. It is the exact opposite of being rude, bitter, harsh and crude. Kindness also involves strength of character that can only be developed, and survive, through practice. Even when kindness is mistreated, it should not end because genuine kindness is not dependent on what the receiver does or does not do. Kindness is strength to be what you should be despite the circumstances.

Kindness is related to wisdom. Again, the supreme example is Christ. Understandably, He encourages us to be God-like: "Love....do good....and you will be the children of the Highest, for He is kind unto the unthankful and evil" (Luke 6:35) and again in Ephesians 4: 31-32 we are encouraged to "***Let all bitterness, wrath, anger....evil thoughts and words, and malice be put away from you. Instead, be kind to each other, be tenderhearted, forgive each other, just as God, for Christ's sake has forgiven you.***" When we do this we are undoubtedly walking on the right track with God.

Kindness does not seek rewards, but because of its nature, rewards are inevitable. The kind person will experience changes in temperament, will feel a sense of satisfaction, and peace. Our personalities change for the better as we allow kindness and love to dominate the spirit of our lives. An enhanced self-concept will continue to evolve as kindness is allowed free expression. Then we are truly moving forward, and towards perfection.

THE GREAT COMMANDMENT

1. Do you obey the commandment to love –
    including yourself?

2. Do you see a clear demarcation between
    loving and hurting yourself?

3. How much do you really love other people –
    including the unlovable?

4. Do you have a role model that shows what
    love is really like?

THE GOOD WALK

*"If you do not know where you are going,
any road will take you there."*
Sterling Holloway

The good walk through life begins with love and its by-products.

We all, even if only subconsciously, want to live a good life, even though we may often mis-define or under-define it. What is the good life? Christ lived it perfectly. He is our prime example. He has set the standards, and has shown that it is possible as a human being to uphold them. In fact it is only in upholding them that we can grow, flourish and become fulfilled.

The task, though practicable, is not an easy one. God knew this and has made available the help that each individual needs. All the tools you need have already been placed at your disposal. They are yours to be used and kept sharp throughout your lifetime. "But unto every one of us is given grace according to the measure of the gift of Christ." (Ephesians 4: 7)

So what are the activities on which we should focus and practise? Instinctively we know most of them, or at least the basic ones. However they are written as constant reminders to all as we continue our journey. St. Paul tells us in Ephesians, chapters four and five, that after we have become "new persons" which God has "created in righteousness and true holiness", we must behave like the new people that we are. He continues by telling us some of the things that we should not return to. These include lying, dishonesty, wrathful active anger, corrupt and unclean conversation and conduct, bitterness and malice, greed and covetousness, sexual promiscuity, and alcohol abuse are some of the things those two chapters deal with. No one will disagree that these are all undesirable, even dangerous habits. St Paul tells us why we should not practise them – they are harmful to us and to others, and he reminds us that "we are members one of another." It is unwise to harm ourselves and others. This is why St. Paul encourages us to be wise. We can do this by going to the source of wisdom, the Bible. There we can gain much useful knowledge for application in our daily lives.

There are many other habits that destroy, instead of building and nourishing the self. These include ingratitude, envy, jealousy, unforgiveness, vengeance, insensitivity, lack of mercy, selfishness and hatred. These are the activities that tend to shrink, harden and stifle the self, as well as cause pain to others. These are the qualities that we all hate to see in other people, but often fail to see them expressing themselves in our own lives. A quality such as ingratitude may seem insignificant and harmless, but it never is. It is always related to other unhealthy features in one's personality. It is related to arrogance and pride and it fails to recognise goodness that is graciously offered.

Living the good life is a process. It is an art that has to be practised. Unhealthy and destructive habits are not always easily abandoned. They will dissipate and release us as we practise and cherish their opposites – the highest of morals, temperance, generosity, forgiveness, kindness, mercy, honesty, selflessness, humility, gratitude etc., etc. In short, we are to practise practical, genuine love.

A CRITICAL LOOK

1. Do you compare yourself with others?

2. Do you set standards for your own life?

3. Are you exactly the same person you were five years ago?

4. Do you have any role models or a source of inspiration and encouragement?

MOULDING THE IMAGE

"Practice is everything."
Periander

At this stage, we can begin to admire and love ourselves more than ever. We can see a bit more clearly the illustrious possibility of what we can become. We can further appreciate our legacy and we can even become excited about moving on and basking in our growth and the eventual fulfilment of the heavenly design for our lives. We have begun to taste real happiness, and of course we want more.

Spiritual health is somewhat like physical health. We must continually take care of it. Neglect always brings unwanted consequences. It is important to take care of ourselves spiritually lest we stagnate along the way. There is much that we can practise to avoid this.

Self-control and discipline are two necessities in every area of our lives. Distractions will always exist and confront us. This is why St. Peter, who knew only too well what it was like to stray and fall, advises us to be sober, to be vigilant, and to resist (1 Peter 5: 8 - 9). Every time we resist doing something detrimental to the self and others, we gain in power and our commitment to pursuing the good life deepens. We grow from strength to strength. The opposite is true. The more we continue to make bad choices, the weaker we become to face the next step. The weaker we become, the more difficult it will be to make the right choices. Unfortunately, there is a destruction point.

What else can we do along the way? St. Paul in the book of Romans, chapter 12 mentions most of what we have already noted, but he adds a few more. He encourages us to cling to goodness and to avoid hypocrisy, to be enthusiastic in God's service. This is important because everything in God's service is designed with our welfare in mind. It is our direction and sustenance along the journey. We are also encouraged to persevere in prayer. This is simply communing with God and keeping in close touch with the One who knows all and loves us to perfection. So we stand to benefit from staying in tune with God. We begin to think like Him, to know His will for our good. We become more and more like Him as the image in us blossoms and flowers.

There is one thing we are told to hate with a passion. This is evil in any form. Remember evil is that which causes pain to the self and to others. This is why we are warned not to render evil for evil, not even to our enemies. The more evil accumulates, the more destructive it becomes. Wherever possible, we must eliminate it, and replace it with love.

St. Paul also places a lot of emphasis on the importance of the way we treat others. He talks about "giving preference to one another." There are times to be utterly selfless, to place others first; and yet in doing so, the self never loses. It becomes free to grow bigger and reach out even more. Think for a moment of the many, many lives that you could affect and brighten with such an attitude.

As we try to live according to the highest of standards, we should of course be very knowledgeable of those standards, and we can never be reminded of them too often. This is the reason we must read the bible in which the way of life is so fully explained. St. Paul, perhaps the most academic of all the apostles, tells us that "**all scripture is given by inspiration of God, and is profitable for doctrine, for reproof, for correction, for instruction in righteousness.**" (2 Timothy 3: 16). St Paul goes further and emphasises why we need to read the bible. The reason is that we "may be perfect, thoroughly equipped to do all good works." How we need it as we travel along! It speaks powerfully to the depths of the heart. "For the word of God is quick and powerful and sharper than any two-edged sword piercing even to the dividing asunder of soul and spirit, of joints and marrow, and is a discerner of the thoughts and intentions of the heart." Isn't this the kind of guide we need always? We can know, beyond any doubt, when we have done wrong. " Thy word have I hid in my heart that I might not sin against Thee," (Psalm 119:11) but when we do, we know that we can be forgiven again and again, and can be refreshed and strengthened for the rest of the journey.

In order for growth to take place, it is not only important to read the bible, but to practise what it teaches. St. James, in chapter 1, reminds us of the lack of wisdom in all those who read but do not practise. They are described as those who see the light but remain unaffected by it. He tells us too of the obvious and certain blessings coming to those who practise the teachings of the Great Book.

As we practise each step, we are carefully fashioning ourselves to conform to the likeness of Christ, our model. This is the self that God is helping us to mould along the journey. It is the perfect Christ-like self in the making, progressing along to its fulfilment.

It is at this stage that we realise we can contribute so much to the beauty of life personally and in general. Our efforts will always, always bring results. We have not only seen the light, but we like it and are walking in it. In short we have begun to share in God's divine power and nature.

WHAT'S YOUR SCORE?

1. Are there things in your life that need changing?

2. Do you have any habits/practices that are harmful to you or others?

3. Are there any qualities that you admire and would like to incorporate into your personality?

4. How can you do that?

WHEN TROUBLE COMES

*"Personality is born out of pain.
It is the fire shut up in the flint."*
J.B. Yeats

Trouble will come! We do not understand why it does, but human life has taught us that we cannot really escape pain and suffering. However it will not break us if we possess a power that is greater than it. In fact, very often we can learn much from it and there seems to be some individually peculiar things that we will not learn without it. In the school of life there are some difficult and painful lessons to be learnt. Having learnt them, we see in retrospect their value to our growth and fulfilment. Like gold, the end product after the testing is truly refined.

But what should be our attitude when trouble confronts us? The first thing we need to remember is that we do not have to face it alone. This is an opportunity to more fully experience the blessings and gifts prepared for us:

power and strength of character, understanding, empathy and forgiveness, patience, faith and trust, humility and perseverance. The list can be longer depending on the trials and the personalities involved. The power of forgiveness is one of the more popular blessings. When one is suffering, one is more likely to be forgiven. Who does not quickly forgive a sufferer? Sometimes we charge such a high price for this very powerful act of forgiveness, one which brings freedom to all those involved – the giver and the receiver.

There are numerous examples of those who have walked safely through the valley and have evolved as wiser, stronger saints, fulfilled. They have all at least one thing in common – a deep faith which causes them never to give up. One psalm writer was driven to ask some soul-searching questions: Will the Lord cast off forever? And will He be favourable no more? Is His mercy clean gone forever? Does His promise fail for evermore? Hath God forgotten to be gracious? (Psalm77: 7-9) The psalmist was able to answer his own questions: "Thou hast with Thine arm redeemed Thy people" Another psalm concludes *"For the Lord God is a sun and shield. The Lord will give grace and glory. No good thing will He withhold from them that walk uprightly. .....Blessed is the man who puts his trust in Thee"* (Psalm 84: 11-12)

The psalms were recorded for their poetic value as well as the lessons we can glean from them. Almost all of them deal with the experience of pain and toil, the sense of falling deep into the valley where there is no friend or relative. But all of them affirm that where everyone else was absent, God was present and man can never truly be alone once He knows an omnipresent God. The key is never to lose sight of such a God no matter how testing the circumstances. This is the time to trust as never before; this is the time when faith becomes " the substance of things hoped for, the evidence of things not seen" ((Hebrew 11:1).This is the experience which will help to equip you with a faith which nothing in the future can threaten. This is the experience in which you can still focus on the Light even though darkness seems to be ever encroaching. This is the time when you feel the excruciating need to cry out to a God of love, and you are hit by the realisation that you are small and helpless indeed, dependent solely on the Giver of Love and grace.

In the end, you can rise to your feet and repeat as so many have done before that "God is our refuge and strength, a very present help in trouble" (Psalm 46:1). You can begin to have a feeling of greater security and even invulnerability. *"The Lord is my light and my salvation. Whom shall I fear? The Lord is the strength of my life, of whom shall I be afraid?" (*Psalm 27:1) *"The Lord is on my side, I will not fear. What can man do unto* me? (Psalm 117:6). This is why we can say with certainty "In the day of my trouble, I will call upon Thee; for Thou wilt answer me" (Psalm 86:7). Then we can say triumphantly *"Great is*

Thy mercy towards me; and Thou hast delivered my soul from the lowest hell." (Psalm 86:13)

Finally we can say with greater determination "I will sing of the mercies of the Lord for ever; with my mouth will I make known Thy faithfulness to all generations."

GIVING UP? OR PRESSING ON?

1. How do you respond to failure and disappointment?

2. Where do you place the blame?

3. Where do you turn for help?

4. Do you know where you can always get the best help to move you forward?

5. What do you do when you experience pain and suffering?

6. Does suffering in the world affect you in any way?

DEEP IN THE VALLEY

Rough wind that moanest loud
Grief too sad for song,
Wild wind, when sullen cloud
Knells all the night long.... **Percy Bysshel Shelley**

"Can I help?"

There are some tough times in our lives, times when we are in a straitened situation, when we hear this question from friends or family and the answer is often a sad, but straightforward "No".

This is the time when we have to face the music alone, in a sense. No one else can take our seat at our desk in the classroom of life. No one else can learn this particular lesson for us. No one else can take this test, pass or fail it for us. It is our very own. We must play out our role on life's stage. We have heard that we must bear our own burdens, carry our own cross, and this is true for each of us even though the burden may be lighter or heavier depending on the individual and the circumstances of the situation. But everyone must pass through the valley.

Passage through the valley seems to be one of life's essentials. It is not dependent on how good or bad a person might be. Christ, our primary example, spent some time there. He felt the loneliness of it all when he asked His disciples if they could not watch with Him for even an hour. His suffering reached peak intensity, not when nails were driven into His hands and feet, but when the loneliness was overwhelming and he actually wondered if God himself had forsaken Him. As a man He experienced a foretaste of what it could be like to be separated from God. However, He died with the assurance that God had not forsaken Him. In fact, God could not forsake Him. Instead, God's presence was manifested to all around and it impacted seriously on some of those who were present. God is omnipresent, so He is always there. We have only to choose to see Him in spite of all the circumstances surrounding us and attempting to block our vision. We have only to embrace Him as he wishes to do to us.

One of the results of Christ experiencing all that He did is to perfect the accomplishment of the mission for which He had taken on manhood. Now mankind everywhere could follow Him, become like Him, triumph as He did and finally become one with Him.

We are fortunate that we can learn so much from the experiences of those who went before us. When I was ill and weak enough to speak only in a whisper, when it took more than eighteen months for me to regain most of my former self, I knew what it meant to be alone, even with a devoted husband present. I felt as if I were in the deepest part of the valley where there was darkness. It was a long and painful experience and I used to wonder when I would be able to walk up the stairs again and return to normalcy. I started to become impatient with my wobbly feet and imbalance. But because of what I had learnt from Christ and His words, I knew that in spite of how alone I felt, God was there. I knew that in spite of the seeming darkness there was Light on which I could focus. This in turn affected my attitude. I looked at myself more critically and opened up my mind to whatever lessons I could eke out of that dark scene in my life.

The lowest point in the valley is when we see ourselves as we truly are and recognize our need of God more than anything or anyone else in this world. The psalmist knew this experience very well and expressed his feelings thus: "My soul longs yea, even faints for the courts of the Lord; my heart and my flesh cry out for the living God" (Psalm 84:2). When this happens, the response we need always comes.

I came out of my experience with a patience that involved greater understanding and empathy. I came out with a greater sense of humility coupled with a deeper appreciation of God's presence and loyalty. This led me to place greater trust in God which increased my own strength and confidence. In short, I had changed. I had grown and I liked what I had become.

During the second year of my experience when I was not yet fully recovered I was suddenly given a mission. I wonder now whether walking in my own valley was not, among other things, to prepare me for that mission.

The four week Christmas holiday for my husband and me was coming to an end and we were both scheduled to return to Rome on the approaching Sunday morning. But the day before, I sat alone on a plane headed, not for Rome, but for Orlando, Florida in the United States!

My sister-in law was ill and needed me, not because she did not have a husband and close family members, but because, according to her, she and I were "more alike".

She had to undergo a series of tests. Then the day came for the doctor to report the results. It was she and I sitting in front of the doctor when he announced that her problem was cancer "which had spread to the bone." The doctor left us alone for a moment and she and I looked fixedly into each other's eyes. I said "You can get through this" and she replied "Yes, I will."

Her walk through the valley began. I spent six months with her, not to walk through the valley with her, because no one really could. But I was there to equip her for the walk. My husband returned to work in Rome as scheduled, and at first I thought that we were sacrificing so much, that I had put my life "on hold". Later I came to understand that my life was not "on hold", but that it was being lived to the fullest, as it was designed for me to live it; that I was growing and responding to a high calling. Then I actually felt honored! I didn't focus on my convalescing health. In fact I realized that I felt stronger and healthier than ever. I was prepared physically and spiritually for the task at hand. I learnt so much from that experience and came out of it a different person.

My first published book, *Reaching for Miracles,* was one of the results. One of the lessons here is that the act of selflessness, by its very nature, always, always impacts gainfully on the doer.

During those six months, Virginia and I made frequent trips to the oncologist and to the Cancer Research Centre for her chemotherapy treatments. In the meantime, we worked at deepening her faith and trust in God. This resulted in a remarkably courageous spirit. She learnt to take one day at a time and to become less and less anxious. She became the patient who counseled and encouraged other cancer patients. The administrative staff admired her and one member commented that Virginia was the most beautiful person she had ever met. Another said that she had never met anyone like her. When she was expected to be very sick from the chemotherapy, she was not. She and I had previously decided, rather boldly, that she would be among the small percentage of people that did not become sick from chemotherapy. Of course she lost her hair, but she and I had gone wig-shopping weeks before. I bought one too. It was meant to be a supportive act as well as to protect my own hair from the harsh winter months.

We acquired and read good books, always looking for something that could be applied in our own lives. There was no reason for the cancer to stop Virginia from growing and becoming what she was designed to be. We are all only in transit and the time we spend here is given to us so that we may learn and grow. The time we are given is adequate for our task. When that development is completed here, we are ready for another dimension. Life here is merely a developmental phase.

Virginia responded well to the treatment, and at the end of six months, I returned to Rome, but we kept in close contact by telephone and e-mail. She continued to grow and I continued to share things from God's word and from my own life. I had given her a diary and encouraged her to write, each day, something for which she could be thankful. In doing so, she discovered that there was a lot for which she was thankful. That diary subsequently made a significant impact on her two daughters.

It is not possible to walk through the valley successfully without putting and keeping on the armor discussed earlier. Virginia used every piece of weaponry available to her as she walked along the path paved with the experiences from which she learnt and grew into what she was meant to be. I too had to be mindful of my armor for own life and to give Virginia the support she needed. In retrospect, I see myself as the angel that God provided for her. She was sure that God had not forsaken her.

"A ROUGH ROAD LEADS TO THE STARS"

1. Have you ever had a very painful experience?

2. Did you learn anything valuable from it?

3. Are friends and family always able to understand and give you all the support you need?

4. Have you tried God as the perfect Father, Friend and Helper?

HOW LONG?

"Patience produces character"
St. Paul

This is the inevitable question for every traveler in the valley. One never knows the answer beforehand, but what is certain is that the walk will never be longer than necessary. Patience is a necessity, whereas anxiety is an obstacle, to quick learning. Anxiety goes hand in hand with fear, and negatively affects the faith and trust that are essential to our growth, our peace of mind and our achievement.

Often we glibly say that patience is a virtue. But some of us are really not convinced about this and many of us sometimes pride ourselves in not possessing it. "I am not a patient person" is one of the confessions that people make so easily as if the lack of it were indeed the virtue. We need the same reminder that St Paul sent to the Romans (Ch5:3-4): ".....***Knowing that tribulation produces patience, and patience produces character, and character, hope; and hope does not disappoint*** *us.....*" This is the kind of patience that remains stoic and trusting in the face of adversity. As William Barclay puts it: "It (patience) is christian steadfastness; that brave and courageous acceptance of everything life can do to us, and the transmuting of even the worst into another step on the upward way." (*Letters of Peter and Jude*).

Patience helps to mould us, to lead us into a security with God that nothing in the valley can truly diminish. God's faithfulness has been a constant theme throughout the ages. One writer exclaims:

"From the end of the earth will I cry unto Thee; when my heart is overwhelmed, lead me to the rock that is higher than I. For Thou has been a shelter for me...." (Psalm 61:2-3).

Time in the valley is not meant to be spent in anxiety, fear, bitterness, worry and despair. Which of these things has ever made the situation better? Each is a potential threat to learning and understanding, and each endangers health. Our attitude and response are most critical at this time. We are still in control and can make the choices that bring peace, happiness and the fulfillment and wholeness that we seek. The purpose of our lives cannot be obliterated because of our experiences. Instead, our experiences help us to fulfill that purpose. Valley time should be the most reflective time of our lives when we , like St Paul, see the wisdom of "*forgetting those things which are behind and reaching forth unto those things which are before, pressing towards the goal for the prize of the high calling of God in Christ Jesus." (Philippians 3:13-14*). This is the time to examine our lives as closely as we can and to measure our success thus far. This is the time to check our sense of direction and determine whether our goals are truly worthwhile and whether we are on course to achieve them.

What are some of the things on which we should focus? St Paul helps us: "...*Whatsoever things are true, whatsoever things are noble, whatsoever things are just, whatsoever things are pure, whatsoever things are lovely....Think on these things."* (Philippians 4:8). These are some of the things which should affect our lives and mould us. One of the results will be peace and empowerment as we grow from strength to strength.

It is true that the valley experience is personal, but this does not mean that help is not provided for us. We all need it. God our Creator has some responsibility for us and He does not shirk His responsibilities, but He needs one thing from us - our cooperation. The writer of Hebrews and many others remind us that we can boldly approach the One who is Love and Compassion and receive "grace to help in time of need." (Hebrews 4:16). We can also be encouraged by believing that we are never given more than we can possibly handle.

Verse 13 of Hebrews chapter 4 states that "all things are naked and open unto the eyes of Him to whom we must give account."

God knows our frailties and our strengths better than anyone else. This is why He has made ample provisions for us. We need only to accept what is offered and always focus on the prize:

"But the God of all grace who has called us unto His eternal glory by Christ Jesus, after that he hath suffered a while, make you perfect, establish, strengthen and settle you." (1 Peter 5:10).

ADULT TRAINING

1. What kind of person are you now? And the next five years?

2. Do you have control over the end product?

3. Do you have a clear concept of the end product?

4. Is there any accessible help?

5. Is there a source of wisdom into which you can tap?

FREEDOM

Morpheus to Neo: "You have to let it all go."
Neo: "Fear, doubt and disbelief. Free
your mind." (The Matrix, 1999)

"And you shall know the truth, and the
truth shall make you free." (John 8:32)

"If the Son therefore shall set you free,
you shall be free indeed." (John 8:36)

We all treasure freedom; we believe it is a basic human right. Most of us, perhaps all of us, believe that we are free. But how free are you? The concept of freedom goes far beyond the physical aspect. We are not free simply because no one owns us as if we were property or because we are not imprisoned. Freedom begins in the mind and it can only meaningfully begin in the right frame of mind, in the right soil so that it can be nurtured to maturity. Enslavement can take on a variety of forms or shapes. We can be enslaved by bad habits, unwise choices, misdirected goals, dishonesty, the practice of lying, deceit, malice, drugs, envy, greed and a host of other things, depending on what drives us to achieve what we consider important.

If these are some of the evil acts with power to enslave us, it follows that in order to be free we must be able to recognize any evil in our lives no matter in what form it appears. The first step then is seeing the truth "and the truth shall make you free", according to Christ who is our ideal example of a free Man, totally unencumbered by anything or anyone. He had a power and an energy to respond to life in ways which seem difficult to comprehend fully. But full comprehension will always elude our finite minds. Instead we are required to exercise elements of trust and faith in One who traveled the road and knows the way; in One who claims to be The Way and the Light - indispensible to us as we travel along.

In seeking to be free from the burdens and entanglements that are obstacles to our growth and fulfillment, we need to accept the help which Christ has graciously offered. We need this help initially as we make that decision to be free and we also need it as we journey. This is so because freedom brings us new challenges and responsibilities. George Bernard Shaw reminds us that "Liberty means responsibility." We become free to be active, to do only those things which result in good physical and spiritual health, free to live the lifestyle which will move us on to full potential and perfection. In short, we become free to so fashion our lives that we become who and what we were designed to be. With freedom comes empowerment. Power is not force or evil. It is the ability to see clearly and act wisely. It is strength of character. We become free to achieve the highest.

"Therefore you are no more a servant, but a son (or daughter). And if you are a son (or daughter), then you are an heir of God through Christ" (Galatians 4:7)

"And if children, then heirs, heirs of God and joint-heirs with Christ"... (Romans 8:17).

OH! OH FREEDOM!

1. Is there anything from which you would like to be free?

2. What is spiritual freedom?

3. How can you obtain it?

4. How can God make you free?

VISION FROM THE MOUNTAIN TOP

"Effort only fully releases its reward after a person refuses to quit." Napoleon Hill

Free at last! Free at last!

This is such a wonderful vantage point. Now we understand and see much more. In retrospect the picture is always clearer and more detailed. We enjoy the sense of freedom from all destructive baggage that we shed along the journey. We are comfortable, happy and full of hope as we contrast our current direction with the one that we abandoned. We begin to taste the triumph over evil and we cherish the persons we have become and are becoming.

Our focus is now more accurate as we accept the advice of St Paul: "If you then are risen with Christ, seek those things which are above…..Set your minds on things above, not on things on the earth" (Colossians 3:1-2).

We can continue to learn what is essentially important and eternally valuable. We can now appreciate our mission more fully and be more determined to accomplish it.

Self assessment and growth become even more prominent in our lives as self development is placed at number one on our priority list. As we work on this, it affects every aspect of our lives. We become more effective parents, better husbands, wives, lovers, partners, colleagues, more efficient employees and employers, and wiser and more useful friends. We are in the process of becoming the best that we possibly can be.

Self evaluation is one of the diagnostic tools we use to spur us on to new and higher levels. As we focus on our growth and keep our eyes on Christ, our Model, we become more eager to move on towards perfection. Therefore we continue to practise the virtues and to add more and more of them to our lives. Surprisingly, we are capable of achieving so much because we have been redirected and are being molded by Christ himself. We can draw from the Source of Power and wisdom.

"In everything you are enriched by Him, in all utterance and in all knowledge." (1 Corinthians 1:5).

This provides the encouragement we need as the horizons to our achievement appear more and more conquerable.

Our confidence can approach its peak as we exercise faith and act upon it.

"…The testimony of Christ was confirmed in you so that you fall short in no gift….. God is faithful by whom you are called into fellowship of His Son Jesus Christ our Lord." (1 Corinthians 1:6&9).

Changes in our lives continue to express themselves. We notice that it is easier to forgive, including ourselves. It is easier to love, not only the loveable but those who desperately need it regardless of what they are. Compassion and kindness flower and bloom in our lives and positively affect the lives of others. Our life is not only a blessing to us, but to others. We are free to function within the human conglomerate as attractors to a better life, instead of creating obstacles in our own pathway as well as in that of others with whom we interact.

The mountaintop is part of our destiny. It is where we are designed to further practice the art of living "until Christ is formed in us." (Galatians 4:19). The practice of loving and being humble helps us to grow rapidly in taking on the form of Christ. Love is the trademark and without it we cannot produce the fruit that helps to fashion us into what we should be:

"Walk in love as Christ also hath loved us and hath given Himself for us…" (Ephesians 5:2).

Such is the nature of love - it gives of the self.

Love is the springboard for many of the qualities we cherish and want to acquire. These include patience and humility which eventually lead to true greatness, goodness, righteousness, and finally godliness.

"Therefore, leaving the basics of the Christian doctrine, let us go on to perfection." (Hebrews 6:1).

You can do all things through Christ who strengthens you!

Dare to believe it!

DID YOU DO YOUR BEST?

1. Are you satisfied that you are doing the best you can?

2. Do you self - check for real growth?

3. Are you any closer to being the "best you"?

4. Is the "best you" your primary focus?

5. Are you seeing more clearly what real happiness is like?

THE LIGHT IS IN SIGHT

1. Where do you get the strength you need to continue your journey?

2. Do faith and perseverance fit into the picture?

3. Does prayer or communing with God help in any way?

4. What kind of answers or solutions are you looking for?

5. Have you made any changes in your life for the better?

BREATHE ON ME

"Breathe on me breath of God,
Till I am wholly yours,
Until this earthly part of me
Glows with Thy fire divine."
(Hymns: Ancient and Modern)

The atmosphere on the mountain is understandably different from that on the plains and the valleys, and it is a difference which intensifies as we move on. Our focus is now more accurate. We focus on a self that is now being more reflective of the omnipotent, omniscient One Himself, and we have come to understand our real worth as the true self continues to emerge, approaching that God-like state.

Now that we can see God much more clearly, we can sharpen and refine our goals as we move towards the completion and the ultimate of our transformation. We are convinced of God's truth about his plan for us, and we are more eager and committed to *"stand fast in the liberty wherewith Christ hath made us free;*

and be not entangled again with the yoke of bondage."
(Galatians 5:1).

St Paul prayed a remarkable prayer for the Christians at
Ephesus:

*"That God would grant you, according to the riches of
His glory, to be strengthened with might by His spirit
in the inner man. That Christ may dwell in your hearts
by faith, that you being rooted and grounded in love
may be able to comprehend with all saints, what is
the breadth and length, and depth, and height, and
to know the love of Christ which surpasses knowledge,
that you might be filled with all the fullness of God.*"

What a prayer! Sounds impossible? And yet we can dare
to say this prayer because this is what the soul longs for.
This is fulfillment in its finest glory. This is the climax of
the legacy- that we would be one with God and Christ.
To be filled with the "fullness of God" opens up limitless
possibilities for us because of who and what God is. If we
try to make a list of words that attempt to say something
about God we can begin to better understand our legacy.
A partial list includes:

Accessible
  Almighty
Brother
  Care

Compassion
> Counselor

Divine
> Enduring

Faithful
> Forgiving

Friend
> Freedom

Grace
> Greatness

Generosity
> Goodness

Guide
> Glory

Helper
> Honorable

Hope

Humble
> Infinite

Immortal
> Invisible

Just
> Joy

Kindness
> Knowledge

Love
> Light

Mercy
> Miracle

Permanence
> **Power**

Prudence
> **Royalty**

Rock
> **Refuge**

Strength
> **Shepherd**

Supreme
> **Spirit**

Truth
> **Trinity**

Wonderful
> **Wealth**

Worthy

And the list is not complete.

Each one of us has always been the focus of such a God. Now He is our focus, so there is the mutuality and the cooperation that is vital to our growth. From this vantage point, all other things fall into their correct places because the foundation and the core have been set right. We are in tune with the Highest Good. We begin to think and act like Him. We are in the process of becoming like Him. We are reminded in 1 John3:9 that "Whosoever is born of God does not practise sin….because he is born of God." This is the new life on which we have embarked. Now we have a sense of true power and we cannot fail.

We understand His plan for us and acknowledge that it is perfect. It was designed with our best interest in mind. Acknowledging this will result in greater appreciation, gratitude, enthusiasm and a determination to stay in close communion with the One who first and unconditionally loved us and Who will do so throughout eternity.

"My Beloved is mine and I am His"

He will present me "holy, and unblameable and unreproveable…" (Colossians1:22).

This sounds like nothing less than Perfection.

This is the goal! The attainable Goal!

"YOU SHALL BE LIKE HIM...."

1. Is there a higher ideal?

2. How hard have you been working towards such an ideal?

3. Is Christ your model whom you try to imitate?

4. Do you realize that even if you fall short, as you will, that Christ will eventually present you flawless?

5. Doesn't that thought spur you on?

You can achieve the goal! That incredible but attainable goal!

EPILOGUE

….So the process of writing this book became an invaluable experience for me. Never before was I so convinced about God's inspiration and leading. Chapter by chapter I wrote on fully assured that I was only the amanuensis. Without any difficulty, the headings, followed by the substance for each chapter evolved. There were times when I reached the end of a chapter and marveled that I had actually written it!

VALLEY TO MOUNTAIN TOP was for me like a spiritual journey, a closer walking with God and working with Him. It resulted in a deeper trust in the Father Who is Love, Who fashions, helps and guides me.

I was truly blessed to have been a secretary guided by God Himself. It is my earnest prayer that others would be blessed by this book and enter a closer Father-Child relationship with such a tremendous and awesome Father and God.